— *from the* **AUTHOR-ITY** *series* —

START WITH THE DRAFT

How to easily plan and write a non-fiction book

Dixie Maria Carlton

First Published 2023
Second Edition Published 2025 by Dixie Maria Carlton

Published by Dixie Carlton Limited
www.dixiecarlton.com
New Zealand

Produced by Indie Experts Publishing & Author Services
www.indieexpertspublishing.com

Copyright © Dixie Maria Carlton 2025

All rights reserved.

The moral right of the author to be identified as the author of this work has been asserted.

No part of this book may be copied, shared, recorded for audio purposes or used for teaching or coaching purposes without the express permission of the author. It may not be stored in a retrieval system, shared or transmitted for public or private use.
'Fair use' of brief quotations embodied in articles may be used with credit to the author, with permission sought.

There may be errors of grammatical or other form; however, the author apologises in advance and assures you, the reader, that every care has been taken to minimise irregularities.

The author and publisher does not purport to be offering advice in legal, accounting, or any other professional services. This content is shared as a teaching process for developing content for the purpose of writing a book. That is all. If you require legal advice or other expert assistance, you should seek the services of a professional.

Cover design by Daniela Catucci
Typesetting & Layout by Ammie Christiansen, Fast Forward Design
Typeset in 11pt Minion Pro

ISBN
Printed: 978-1-7386102-6-6

Here's to all the writers who ever wanted to express themselves with beautiful words, heartfelt phrases and stories; to have their words make a positive difference in the world in which we live. Keep writing and helping others to understand that which you are able to articulate for them by making the complex simple, the ugly beautiful, and the meaning clear so they may rest easy in what they read today.

Dixie Carlton

How to Use this Book

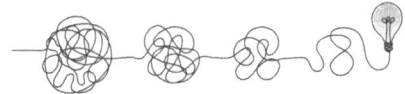

This simple book is packed with resources, guidance and tools to help you think about your book, plan its contents, and finish your first draft so it's ready for testing with beta readers, and then for final editing.

It's not about how to produce the book, format it, design it, or any of that other information you will eventually need. This is called Start with the Draft because that's what you need to do. By following the process laid out in this book, you might save on a lot of structural editing and become confident in both your book's readability and the joy your readers will get from it.

Along the way, you'll find extra invitations to reach out to me if you get stuck and to 'do things' as you progress. Think of this book as being like your Non-Fiction Writing Coach, because that's what I do, and this is the information I share every day with authors just like you.

Contents

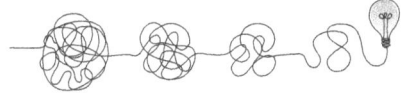

How to Use this Book	4
Introduction	7
Part 1 — Before you start writing your book	10
Dear Author	11
Impostor Syndrome	15
You have to <u>Think</u> about your Book!	19
The Tri-Variant Framework ™ (TVF)	25
Creating a Book Plan Using The TVF	27
How Many Chapters?	35
FAQs, Fun Facts & Case Studies	39
Manuscript... Next Steps	41
Using a Plan to Write	43
Writing a Book Pitch	47
Part 2 — Writing Your First Draft	53
First...the BIG Question of Size	55

Writers Block	57
Word vs Google Docs	59
Sharing Your Work	61
Titles & Subtitles	63
Perfection Kills Creativity	67
Writers are Readers	69
Author Quicksand	71
Pre-formatting Your Manuscript	75
Review Your Draft	81
Your Test Pilots	83
Front and Back Matter	87
What to do next...	89
Call to Action	91
Acknowledgements	93
Extra Resources	94
About Dixie Carlton	95

Introduction

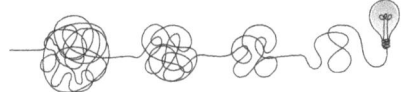

I wrote this book just for you, you who yearns to write a book yourself but feels a little overwhelmed by the whole idea. I mean, I know when I wrote my first book, I had no idea where to start or what to do, and so I did what most first-time authors do: I simply started putting words into a blank document on my computer. Then some refining was needed – loads of it! My mind hounded me with endless questions about whether I had written too much or not enough, or whether my sentences even made sense. And then, after obsessing endlessly about what I'd written, new questions sprang up about what to do once I'd finished all that writing. These were the questions that plagued me as I wrote, refined, and repeated these steps endlessly over several months before finally deciding it was time to ask a graphic designer friend to help me make it 'look good'.

I had created a book... *and it was truly dreadful.* With the benefit of having worked for many years on hundreds of other books, I can see now that I made a complete mess of that first book. But it did get me a paid trip to Las Vegas, where I spoke at a conference, met with other speakers, and started to learn just how much I needed to learn if I was going to have any semblance of a career as an expert at something.

So, I set about learning all I could and came to understand exactly how much the professional speaker industries and non-fiction publishing industries are intertwined. Suddenly, I was helping other speakers to write and publish their books.

That was at the start of the revolution of what is now known as publishing 3.0.

Let me explain....

Publishing 1.0 was when Guttenberg developed the printing press, opening reading and writing to the world beyond the church and nobility.

Publishing 2.0 started when e-books and digital content was made easier to produce. But quite frankly, that heralded in the age of an awful lot of rubbish books being dumped on the market, and suddenly 'everyone' being an author.

Every second person you'd meet at speaker conferences would have a book to thrust at you. Sadly, there are now many million-dollar speakers walking around with business cards disguised as 10-dollar books.

Just because technology makes it possible to record a lot of content and magically have it printed in a matter of weeks does not mean doing that is a good idea. It's akin to wearing beautiful, silky underwear under your daggy sweatpants!

Publishing 3.0 is about producing high-quality content across multiple platforms, but it starts with a great book. And planning a great book means working out who your market is and what they need from you.

Discerning recipients of information want the good stuff.

Great speakers need books as a significant part of their marketing ecosystem, not a stand-alone item that does nothing more than end up on a dusty bookshelf and fails to generate more than a handful of opportunities for the author.

I've now worked with more than 200 authors. Most of them are

professional speakers, and many of them are multi-award-winning and/or best-selling authors too. And they all have two things in common: they doubted their ability to write an excellent book, and they used lack of time as an excuse not to do it.

Like me with my first books, they didn't know how to get their books working hard for them. They had no idea where to start or how to get their best content out of their heads and into the hands of their target market.

Getting real leverage from your best content starts with getting it curated and well written in a book that can then be used across multiple platforms such as social media, blogs, articles, and reports you can inspire your market with.

If you want to avoid having a marketing tool that is effectively an expensive business card loosely disguised as a book, then you need to start here. Focus on getting the best material you have into a book that people really want to read – one that is crafted well, edited to the highest standards, and designed and produced to exacting quality.

*But first, let's deal with the content. This book is about that. There are other books about what to do with it **once you're past the first draft stage**.*

Part 1

Before you start writing your book

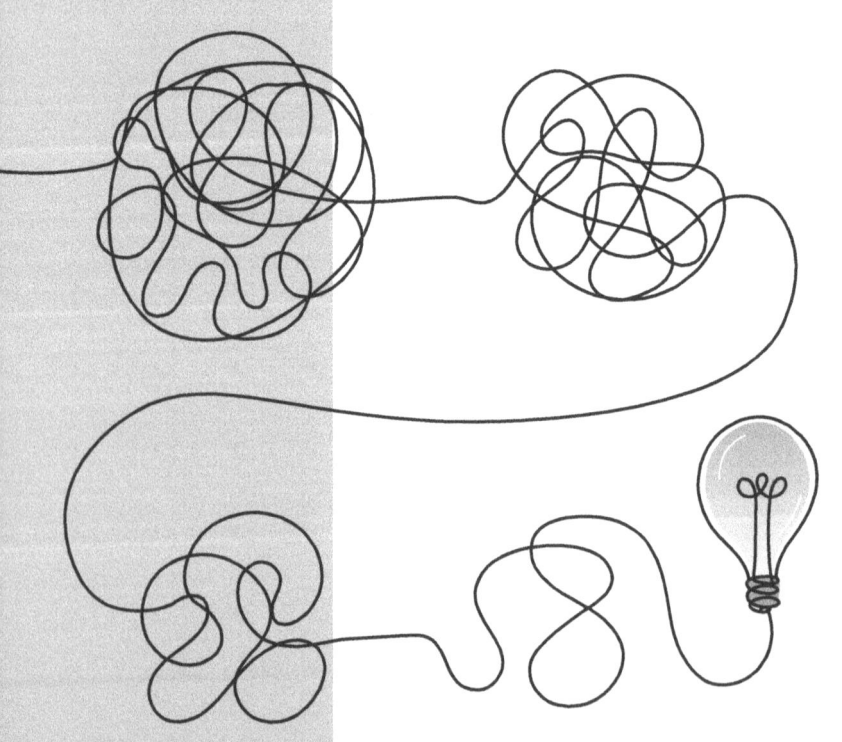

Dear Author

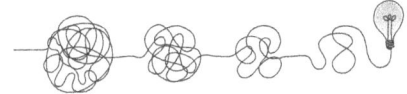

Firstly, congratulations on wanting to take your brilliant ideas, experiences, and wisdom to a new dimension and deciding to write the book you've been thinking about, and maybe even talking about, for a while now.

You're probably wondering where to start. You're probably agonising over questions like, Will I have time to do it well? Will I be able to maintain momentum on this type of project? Will anyone bother to read what I wrote anyway? Is it worth it?

Well, yes. Writing a book is the very best way to ensure your specialist expertise is verified in your industry.

I'll get to what you need to do to make it easy on yourself shortly. But first, I really want you to know that I believe in you. You got this. And I'm here to help you get your book out of your head and into the hands of your readers so it works hard for you.

Dixie

Let's Talk about WHY
You Want to Write this Book

Why you, why now, why this book, why… why… why??

My mother used to berate me for always starting a conversation with "WHY". I was exceptionally curious as a child and that curiosity has only increased with age. I want to know everything about anything that even slightly piques my interest. But the issue of 'why' as it relates to marketing, business, and you writing this book is a critical matter to discuss.

If you're here reading this book, you're likely doing so because you know it's time to have a book that serves as a serious part of your marketing ecosystem.

What will a book do for you?

- For your business?
- For your future career prospects?
- For your readers?

As either a professional speaker, merchant of knowledge, industry expert, or simply as someone who thrives in the face of great adversity, your book is going to impact on you just as much as on your readers. This is because as you go through the development and writing of it, you'll gain an even clearer perspective on your own wisdom and experiences.

You have a choice as to how you create this book and how you want it to fit into your overall marketing strategies. You could turn it into an e-book with an associated workbook, training manual, audio book, or print version.

You may want to develop a podcast or a series of YouTube videos and use this as the linchpin that holds those things together. You may even have those other platforms already covered, and your book is just the last thing to add to the mix.

Maybe you just want to share what happened to you and why you it's important others learn from your personal story. These are all equally valid reasons to write a book.

So, spend a moment thinking about *what this book is really going to do for you*. Will it open doors for you to speak at events, training sessions or conferences? Perhaps it will justify raising your fees for work you're already doing in that space. Or maybe you need to have a book to use as a lead magnet to sell your other services.

Once you know *why* you want to write this book, it's important to address *how* you can make it a reality, and this book is just the start of that journey. It's also very important to note that if you are going to have this book represent your brand and be a bold servant to help achieve those things, then you must consider the value of your brand before you even start.

Yes, it's possible to spend a few days recording a lot of information before it's sent off to be transcribed, quickly edited, have a cover slapped on it and then uploaded to Amazon, but that does not mean it's a good idea.

Technology makes so much of what we do easy. But if you're wanting to save yourself being criticised for a substandard effort, then listen up. *Please.*

Your book needs to be edited, designed, and formatted professionally if it's going to be valuable to anyone.

Maybe you have the skills to write and curate your content well, in which case this book is all you need to write something of immediate value to others. But you also have the option to bring in writing help if you need it.

Beyond writing and crafting this first draft, you will likely need help with editing, design, social media, and publishing. Once your intentions to write are confirmed, start to think about your team (as mentioned in the next couple of pages) and identify who you will work with as your editor, coach, design team, and publishing team, so that you can be assured of a high-quality, brand-worthy book that really works hard for you.

This **part is just the beginning.**

Now, let's talk about the biggest challenge most authors have: confidence. Let's start by addressing your worries and putting that imposter syndrome firmly where it needs to be.

Impostor Syndrome

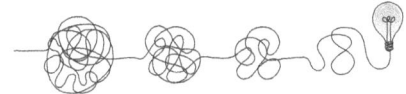

Let's Call Him Boris!

Give your imposter syndrome a name so we can address them directly and remind them who's really the boss of you – *and it sure ain't Boris!* Right?

Boris likes to hang about and tweak your calm sense of well-being just when you're feeling proud of yourself and ready to do something big. Maybe he's the voice of your parent, grandparent, school bully, or horrid cousin. It doesn't matter who you hear because everyone has a Boris, and he says exactly the same shit to everyone, and it really is *shit*! Why waste time listening to those repetitive self-doubts about not being good enough to do this. You may think, 'who am I to write this book?' *Who are you NOT to do this?* How do you serve the world by being smaller than you really are? You have these experiences, this wisdom, and the desire to help others by sharing it. That's maybe why you had all those things happen in your life – so you can use them for the benefit of someone else.

So, here's what to do with Boris while you're writing your book.

Remind them that they have not personally written a book themselves, ever, and so how could they possibly know what you're capable of doing. If they'd like to pop off and do their own book project before coming back to you and mocking your efforts, they'd better have good reason – and one million sales of their own – before harassing you with your as-yet unborn book baby. In other words, tell your imposter syndrome avatar that this is *your* project, and your ability to do this might depend on other people to help you, but that's okay. You're ready for that, and you don't have to do this alone.

This is not a solitary experience. It takes a village to raise a child and a team to produce a high-quality book. *And your book deserves to be high quality.*

A quick note on the resources in this book.

You'll find several great resources in here, and if you want to use them as you find them in 'small size', then please, feel free. Or you can take a photocopy and increase the size, print them out, or re-create your own version. You can even grab them as a stand-alone item on my website if you haven't already.

Here's the link:

www.indieexpertspublishing.com/startwiththedraft

Getting the manuscript well crafted is important. It makes the reader experience a lot better and gives you a great flow of content you can use in addition as social media posts, articles or blogs.

There is a lot more to do after you've written your manuscript, tested it, refined it and made it ready for editing. But there are other books and resources I have referenced for you at the back of this book for that stage of your authority journey.

Taking Your Temperature

As we work through this book, you're going to have moments where you want to just race off and get into it, and that's fine. But you'll also do well to slow down and work through the entire book first, then maybe mark bits to come back to and work through fully.

You're also going to blow hot and cold on the whole idea of writing this book as the enormity of it unfolds and you find Boris occasionally poking at you from the sides of your mind too. Tell him to bugger off, and then take a deep breath. But we'll also work through a few temperature checks as we go too, so you can identify exactly what might be holding you back and where your strengths are. Let's do that now.

Rate each question on a 1–5 basis:
5 being VERY much YES, and 1 being NO, not really!

I know I'm ready because:

I have a topic I'm truly passionate about.	
I am frequently told I should write a book about my topic.	
I have enough knowledge to write at least one book about this.	
My book will be a brilliant marketing tool for me to use in my work.	
I can devote at least 2–4 hours per week to this project for the next 6 months.	
My social media platforms are well populated with people I can promote my book to.	

I find it easy to write content/blogs/articles.	
The thought of doing this keeps me up at night – I'm so excited about writing this book.	
I know this book will help a lot of people.	
I have a coach or cheerleader to help me with this project when it gets challenging.	

Add up your scores and see which of these applies best to you.

1–15: You're going to need to read this entire book and think hard about why you want to write a book. Really consider what you want this book to do for you and your career. You may be ready to work through the first three chapters, but you're not actually ready to do your book planning yet.

16–35: You're going to find the next few pages very helpful and you're ready to do a book plan, but you will benefit from working with a coach or advisor to help you stay focused and see this project through to its completion.

36–50: You're ready and able to get this project started. You have a burning desire to do what needs to be done to make a success of this project. You're going to love this process as we take your ideas and turn them into high-functioning content that you can use as part of your marketing ecosystem.

Now that you're clear on what might be holding you back and how ready you really are to get going with this amazing project, we're going to roll up our sleeves and do the hardest part of all. The most important step in this journey is this:

YOU HAVE TO <u>THINK</u> ABOUT YOUR BOOK!

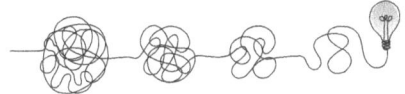

Yes, the thinking part is the hardest part. But it's also critical because EVERYTHING else comes from this one important step. It's like deciding to take a trip up the mountain and not knowing what to pack into your backpack in order to remain hydrated, fuelled, dry, and to not get hopelessly lost if you wander off the path.

The thinking part of this journey is simple, but that does not necessarily mean it's easy. It is also the part that is going to keep you on track and get your content written in record time, with the all-important call to action at the end of your book. You need to be sure your reader can act at the end if they want more of you and what you have to share with them. There's really not much point in writing this book without a call to action unless it's a fiction story and you're writing it for entertainment purposes only. But even a memoir is likely to be shared because you want to inspire your reader in some way – even if it's just to follow your Instagram posts for additional inspiration.

DON'T rush through this... Take time to really think about who your readers are!

Please start working through your answers to this information before moving on to writing a book pitch.

Resource Reminder – you can easily access the full set of templates featured in this book, and some bonus ones too, simply by visiting: www.indieexpertspublishing.com/startwiththedraft.

WORKSHEET #1

Before you start to write your book draft

Take your time with these questions. When you ahve finished answering them, write a 500 word description about your book.

Why do you want to write a book, this book, why now?

How do you want this book to affect your life/career/business?

Who is your ideal reader? What do you know about them?

What action do you want the reader to take after reading this book?

Describe the size, length, type of book this will be?

Are there other similar books in this genre? Do you know your competition?

© Dixie Carlton 2025 All Rights Reserved.

This worksheet, and your book pitch, are two vital things to get right *before* you start writing a book.

If downloading the worksheet is not your thing right now, grab a pen and paper instead and find a quiet place to work through these important questions.

Why are you writing this book?

What do you want to have happen when you complete it? Do you want to change the world; start a revolution; inspire fresh thinking in your industry; get called up for coaching, training, or speaking – or something entirely different? The next lesson on defining your purpose will help with this a lot. Because it's such a big thing, start thinking about it before turning the page.

Why is NOW the time for you to write this book?

Is there something coming up (e.g., an anniversary, business opportunity, or pending change in a political issue) that will impact the timing of this book? Whatever it is, consider how much time is available to you to meet that (self-imposed) deadline. Are there other factors that can impact on the timing for its release? Is there something in your own career pathway that makes *now* the right time to do this?

How do you want this book to impact on your career?

Will you use this book to start or boost your speaking career, or will you want more bookings as a trainer or coach? Decide on what you want to have happen for you as the author; then you'll know how to position your very important call to action. The call to action is what you want to 'breadcrumb' throughout the book to ensure people take the action you want.

What do you want to tell your reader to DO when they finish reading this book?

Guide them towards your call to action by telling them throughout the book what you wish to inspire them to do. Is it to call you? Do you want them to start a revolution, take up a hobby, research something further, or just tell their friends about your book? I'd recommend not relying on that last one. If you simply want to write it because you want to write it, well, go right ahead. But your deeper and more meaningful purpose behind this book will keep you focused, drive your momentum to finish it, and serve your readers well when they read it.

What will it look and function like?

Think about things like its size, length, images, workbook, quotes, photos, and anything special to make it stand out. Will it be a manual, coffee table book, a memoir or an inspirational book?

Take time to answer these questions and then write a book pitch (see page 47). You might think that these are only for working with agents or traditional publishers, but the reality is these will sharpen your awareness of who your market is. Know who is competing for the same readers, what makes your book different from theirs, why your book is important, and what you bring to this topic as an expert. If you enter this process without these bits of knowledge firmly in your mind, it *will* make everything so much harder for you when it comes time to review your work. Save yourself time now, and get it done.

This was the first part of your planning, the *pre*-planning. You need to get clear on all those things in order to move on to the next part: Content Planning.

Resource Reminder – you can easily access the full set of templates featured in this book, and some bonus ones too, simply by visiting: www.indieexpertspublishing.com/startwiththedraft.

Don't Stay Stuck!

If you're struggling to get through this starting point, or somewhere along the way you just wish someone would do this for you, then here's your solution: talk to us. My team and I do this every day.

We get that not everyone wants to, or is able to, devote the time and skills required for writing their own book. But that doesn't mean you have to hold back on getting your content out there. Schedule a time to talk with us about what you need the most help with.

Dear Author,

Please, don't feel stuck or overwhelmed…

I know precisely how hard it can be to plan everything from wherever you might currently be on your journey. We're here to help. If you need to explore options for how to prioritise all these parts of your journey, have a conversation with me or one of my amazing team members and get real clarity about the journey ahead. We can even do a lot of the heavy lifting, including the writing, for you.

This is what we do every day for authors at all stages of their journey, just like you.

I've personally worked with more than 200 authors, and their books, many of which are now best sellers. I've worked to make my clients high-profile experts in their industries. I know the speaking and the publishing industry and how they intersect particularly well. So, let's have a chat about your aspirations.

Dixie

THE TRI-VARIANT FRAMEWORK ™ (TVF)

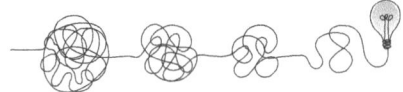

Three is one of my favourite numbers. Maybe I just like curves and squiggles, but I choose to believe it's a little deeper than that, and my fascination with triplets is derived from how frequently the number three appears in our lives.

From Pythagorean theorems to conversational structure, to comedy and atomic structure, the number three exists in almost everything we do.

Think about the **Rule of Three** as it's applied in nearly every fairy tale you ever read. The *three* blind mice, the *three* little pigs, the *three* quests to find the key/save the princess/overcome the /monsters.

Why do we use three so much?

Because something's more easily remembered when we do. It's the lowest number from which to form a pattern and patterns are easy to see and recall. Three is such a memorable number that many ancient mythologies adopted it in huge swaths of lore.

In professional speaking, we use the concept of 'tell them what you're going to tell them, tell them, then tell them what you told them' as a framework for developing a presentation.

This Tri-Variant Framework™ is one I've been developing and refining over many years and hundreds of books, articles, speeches, and stories. It works. And it's a bit like putting a jigsaw puzzle together when you use it.

It consists of three parts divided into three chapters, which further divides into three parts per chapter – at least for the initial planning stages. The finished result may vary from that structure, but this is primarily about getting the information into some usable structure. I'll explain what I mean further in the 'How Many Chapters' chapter.

Creating a Book Plan Using The TVF

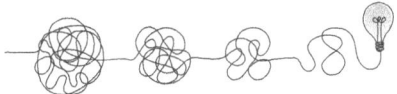

When thinking about your book topic in a general sense, can you identify three primary sub-topics?

For example, if it is a book about business, then maybe you could use sales/marketing/finance. Here are some other examples of sub-topics to get you started.

Business:
- sales/marketing/finance
- hiring people/training/management
- branding/advertising/marketing
- customers/service/loyalty programs

Education:
- primary/secondary/tertiary schools
- high school/career planning/study skills

Relationships:
- dating/marriage/divorce

Travel:
- packing/planning/my travel blog
- Asia/Africa/America

TVF WORKSHEET #2

Planning your Contents

Identify THREE main sections of your book - what is each one about?

Part 1:	*Part 2:*	*Part 3:*

Break each of the three sections down into THREE main Chapters.

Part 1			
Part 2			
Part 3			

Now break those down into THREE - these will become your sub-headings per chapter.

(*Map this out on a white board, draw up on a large grid plan, or use our downloadable worksheet*).

© Dixie Carlton 2025 All Rights Reserved.

Part & Chapter Mapping

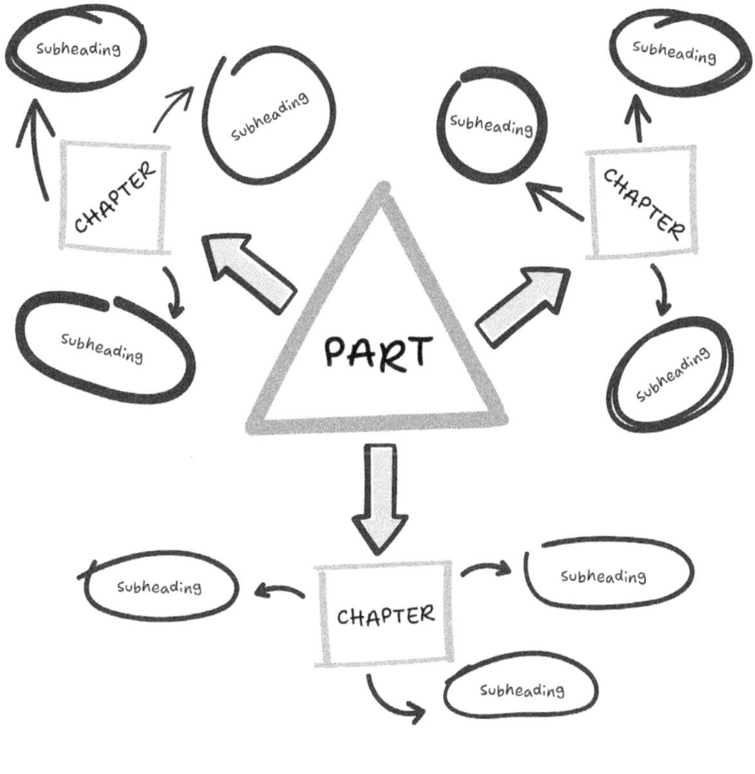

Book Plan

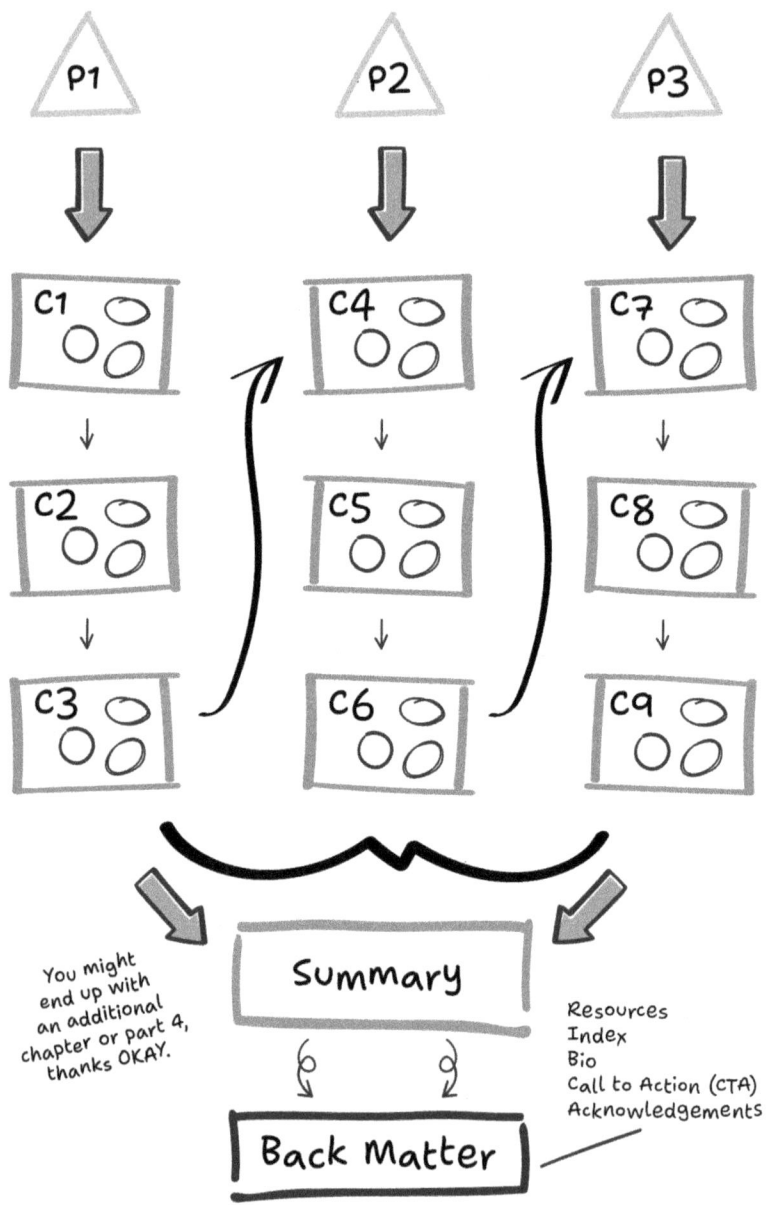

Keep it simple at this stage. Focus primarily on the THREE PARTS and subsequent THREE CHAPTERS for each. Break each of those three chapters down into (approximately) THREE SUBHEADINGS per chapter.

You may end up with an additional chapter or part 4 at this stage. That's okay. Or you might use the flow chart concept (as shown here) to include your notes about the summary and back matter (such as references, a glossary or an index). But mostly, you are aiming to work within the Tri-Variant concept of three parts, each with three chapters, each with three subheadings.

Your 9–10 chapters, each made up of three sections, can easily translate into 30 posts or articles and captions for memes to share on your social media. There is an additional resource I've created for you to do that once you've finished this part. Please check the link at the end of the book for more information.

When you've finished with the overall chapter plan, transcribe it onto a colourful card with Post-it notes and keep it handy every day, adding to it as you need to. Write all over it, highlight bits, customise and utilise it as often as you need to.

Remember – this is a working document!

Download your own copy of this worksheet **FREE** at

www.indieexpertspublishing.com/startwiththedraft.

Book Plan Example - Business Book

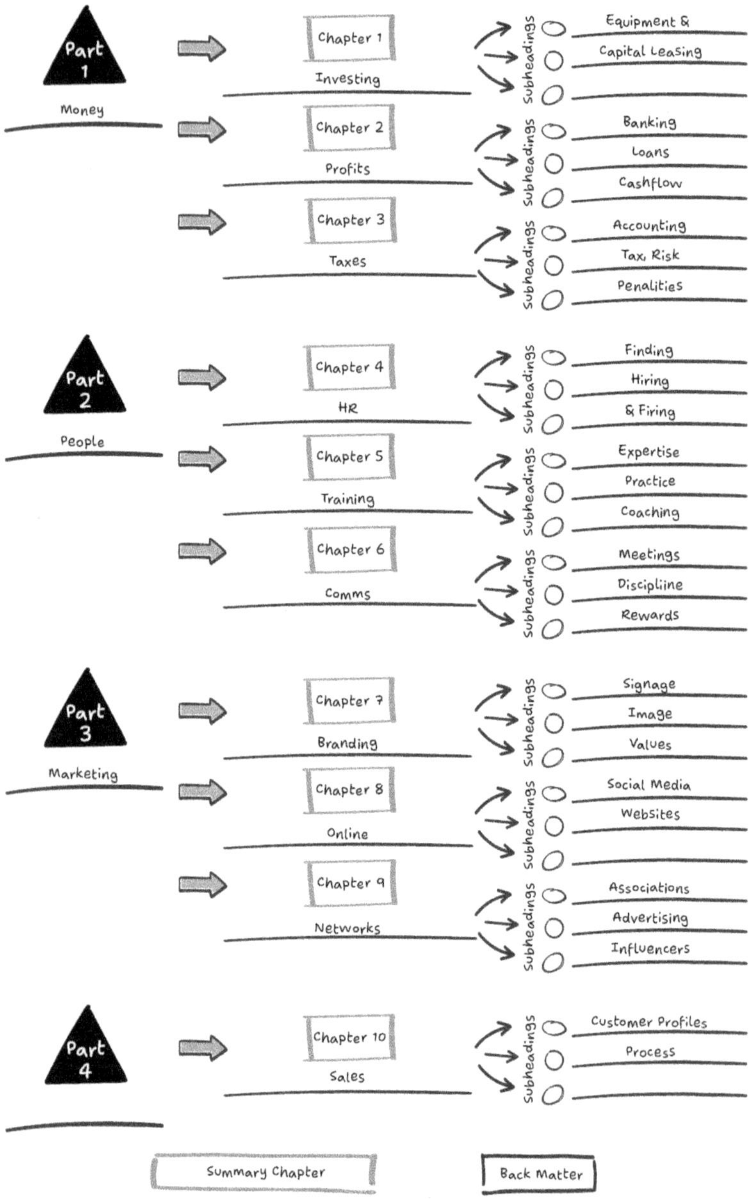

Part 1 — Money

- Chapter 1: Investing
  - Subheadings: Equipment & Capital Leasing
- Chapter 2: Profits
  - Subheadings: Banking, Loans, Cashflow
- Chapter 3: Taxes
  - Subheadings: Accounting, Tax, Risk, Penalities

Part 2 — People

- Chapter 4: HR
  - Subheadings: Finding, Hiring, & Firing
- Chapter 5: Training
  - Subheadings: Expertise, Practice, Coaching
- Chapter 6: Comms
  - Subheadings: Meetings, Discipliine, Rewards

Part 3 — Marketing

- Chapter 7: Branding
  - Subheadings: Signage, Image, Values
- Chapter 8: Online
  - Subheadings: Social Media, Websites
- Chapter 9: Networks
  - Subheadings: Associations, Advertising, Influencers

Part 4

- Chapter 10: Sales
  - Subheadings: Customer Profiles, Process

Summary Chapter | Back Matter

Now it's your turn

- What are the three PARTS of your book?
- What chapter heading would you give each part?

Lay your answers out in a grid similar to the one in the example. Note that each line in your grid is a part/theme/section in the same order the chapters will appear in your book. This is about *Reader Flow*. Start at the beginning and work through to the middle, then get to the end.

Think about which stories, facts, examples, or statistics you might want to put into each chapter and write those into the relevant chapter squares.

Now, focus on what each chapter might break down into and give each of those a subheading.

Think about what your Introduction will say. Generally, this is a 'letter to your reader' explaining what the book is about, and perhaps even why you wrote it to them.

A summary chapter might also be included, but you can leave that until after you've written the introduction and core chapters.

There will be other parts to your completed manuscript, and we will cover things like your bio, acknowledgements, foreword, and your call to action. But for now, you just need to get this chapter outline done.

TAKE YOUR TIME on this!

**It's important to plan as thoroughly as possible _before_ you start writing your manuscript.
This will save you on writing time and structural editing.**

How Many Chapters?

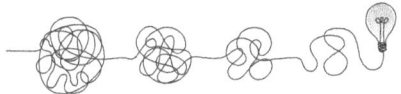

I've given you a four-part example but I recommended starting with a three-part plan. Let me explain.

Ideally, you want to think about the start, middle, and end, or, A, B, C. To give a fairy tale example: (a) the princess needs to marry a prince, (b) there is a quest for the prince, and (c) finally the prince and princess meet and live happily ever after. Stories generally work well in three parts. We're sort of wired to expect and appreciate three parts in books and plays.

But you may find some things lend themselves to an additional chapter, or your summary area might be in three parts; for example, the conclusion or recap chapter, the case studies, and the recommendations.

An Extremely Important Point:

It's called a Tri-Variant Framework™ because your end result may vary from the initial three-by-three framework. The point is that this is how to start planning your draft. It is the simplest way to organise your thoughts about your book into a flow that works for your reader. Some authors like to start with just a list of chapter headings and write from there, but that does not necessarily lead to a flow of content that makes sense.

Remember this, if at any point your reader gets confused or

stumbles over the content, your book is more likely to end up as another in the pile of half-read books beside their bed.

I prefer to start with three parts, then divide those into three chapters, write an introduction and summary chapter, and then split some of those very long chapters into two, if necessary.

Your book is likely to end up as either a series of three core themes divided into their three parts (chapters), and then subheadings with two or more topics. If each of those topics is around 800 words, (a good size article length), then three per chapter, multiplied by 9–12 chapters, works out at a book with 25,000–35,000 words, or between 140 and 200 pages.

There's another point to think about here. You might envision the ideal book as being about 400 pages. Or you might have already written a messy draft of 60,000 or 100,000 words. Consider this: you could unpack that amount of content into two or three separate books – each around 25,000 words – or one book that is around 40,000 words. (A messy first draft is likely to be cut down in word count.) Either way, starting with this process of planning your content is going to save you a lot of writing time, and likely a lot of editing time too.

TVF GUIDE - WORD COUNT

Chapter Breakdown

Part 1	Chapter 1	Chapter 2	Chapter 3
2-3 subheadings per chapter = approx. 2500 words per chapter	700-800	700-800	700-800
	700-800	700-800	700-800
	700-800	700-800	700-800
Part 2	**Chapter 4**	**Chapter 5**	**Chapter 6**
Approx. 2500 words per chapter = Approx. 25,000 words per book	700-800	700-800	700-800
	700-800	700-800	700-800
	700-800	700-800	700-800
Part 3	**Chapter 7**	**Chapter 8**	**Chapter 9**
Approx 25-30K words per book = approx 140-180 pages	700-800	700-800	700-800
	700-800	700-800	700-800
	700-800	700-800	700-800
Part 4	**Chapter 10**	**Summary**	**Back Matter**
Finished size will depend on final formatting, but 5.5x8.5in (140x216mm) = approx 10mm spine	700-800	1000-2000	Resources, Index, Bio, CTA, Acknowledgements
	700-800		
	700-800		

Important Note:

Part 4 maybe just the summary, and the back matter. You may or may not end up with overflow chapters.

If you end up with 9, 10 or 12, or 15, it is irrelevant at this stage. Get the concept of this plan - don't get hung up on the details.

FAQs, Fun Facts & Case Studies

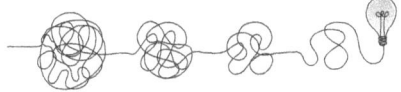

When it comes to deciding what to put into your draft manuscript, you need to use fun facts and case studies to add interest and break up the text a bit. Visually, page after page of paragraphs can look dull. You can use fun facts or commonly asked questions you know are of value to your reader as pull quotes. Put them into side bars or special paragraphs, or have them massaged by your typesetter when you are ready to produce your book to make the pages more stylish.

Work through some of these options as part of your book plan. What are you most often asked about at work, dinner parties or when meeting new clients? What fun facts are there about your business that make interesting 'Aha' moments? Add these to your book.

Short attention spans are rife among readers of all genres these days, so making it easy for a reader to rest on something visually refreshing when turning a page is a very good idea.

You can also use case studies and make them sit inside shaded, boxed areas or frames. Maybe even just format them differently so that they stand out. You might like to access the FREE 'How to write stories and case studies' resource I have listed at the back of this book for clever ways to write and present case studies, stories and examples.

Manuscript... Next Steps

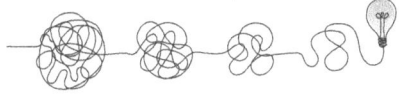

Once you have several chapters written, it's worth turning your collection of independent articles into a document that brings them together in a way that helps you see this as a 'book', not just a set of pages with headings. It makes the book more real to your test readers and helps you see what the chapters will look like. This is also where you can ensure that anything the designer needs to highlight or format in a special way is made clear, so that they do not have to do a lot of guesswork about such things. When you're paying people by the hour to make your book look amazing, ensure they have all the necessary information right off the bat.

A preformatted manuscript also helps you to see where there are places to put images, diagrams, or coloured sections.

There is more about preformatting later in this book, with specific tips, but *this is worth repeating.*

Pssst...
Here's a bonus secret insight!

When you work with a designer to have the typesetting sorted, they will likely use a program called InDesign (this book was typeset using it by our in-house Designer). InDesign is specifically for book production and interacts very well with all options for file preparation – both production of finished digital files and printed options.

You can produce and publish an e-book using just a Micsosoft Word file, but it's best to have it designed and formatted by a professional who knows what they're doing using all the resources and tools available to them.

This is also a simple example of how to build extra visual interest in your book by breaking up the regular text: with a text box.

Using a Plan to Write

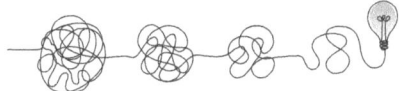

Take your plan, write the chapter outlines on yellow sticky notes, then laminate the whole plan. Put it where you can see it every day, and mark off chapters as you write them, adding notes and ideas as you go. Make it big enough to put on the wall in your office and keep bringing the project to life.

In your planning process, you will have worked out who your ideal reader is and what you want them to *know* and then *do* because of reading your book. The hardest part is sometimes sticking to that.

Create your plan in a way that you can print it out and have it in front of you during your workday so you see it constantly, even when working on other things. Ponder on it often, whenever your eyes need a break from screens, or when you're on boring calls. I also recommend laminating it once you're happy with this first draft plan, so you can write on it with your marker pen, tick off parts when done, and use extra sticky notes to help expand your ideas when needed. Most of these plans do end up quite messy as we go, but that's a great creative way to work through a project like this.

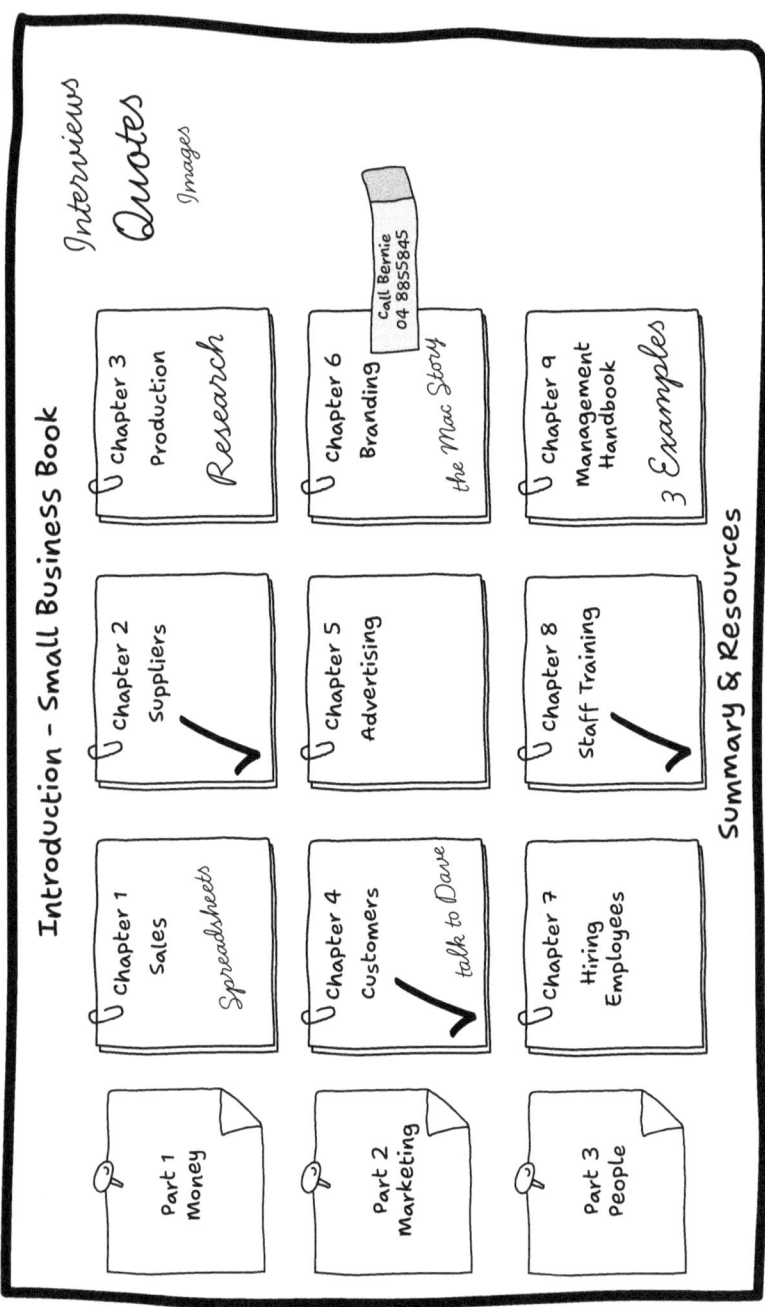

Let's take your temperature

Rate each question on a 1–5 basis:
5 being VERY much YES, and 1 being NO, not really!

My Preperation is Complete because:

My topic easily falls into three main parts.	
I believe my chapters will be easy to write.	
I have enough content to easily write approximately 2,000–3,000 words per chapter.	
I am not going to need to do a lot of research to complete this book.	
I have time to write at least 2,000 words (or one chapter) per week for the next three to four months.	
I have three people I can get support from as I write, who will help test my draft content.	
I am clear about my call to action.	
I am clear about why this is the right time to write this book.	
I know exactly who my target market is and what they will want from this kind of book.	
I am certain of the reasons I want to write this book and how it will assist my career and marketing strategy in the future.	

Add up your scores and see which of these applies best to you.

1–15: You might want to go back to your preplanning and get some help from a coach to gain clarity around these areas. You may also benefit from working with a co-writer or ghost writer to move you forward on this.

16–35: You're mostly ready and able to get this project off the ground. Writing the pitch document will help clarify some of what you feel you're missing at this stage, and your confidence might be the only thing holding you back. Talk with a coach or mentor about some of the things you feel you're not quite ready to tick off yet.

36–50: You're ready, so let's get you moving forward and starting to write your first draft.

Writing a Book Pitch

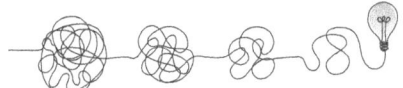

It's a good idea to write a pitch document, so I've included this as an option. If you're impatient to get started, circle back to this by all means. But at some point, you will need to do this as it's the commercial end of your planning.

A pitch tells the publisher/reader why they should read your story, whereas a synopsis (more commonly used in fiction) answers the question 'What is the story?' If you can't write a decent 3,000-word book pitch and synopsis, you are probably going to struggle with writing a great book. You do not need any fancy programs to start your book pitch; just write it up in a Word document and follow these simple steps.

If you are pitching your book proposal to a literary agent or traditional publisher, these are the parts you will need to cover and the questions they will have. However, some of these points are also critical for you to work through as part of your overall planning beyond simply what the book is about.

Working Title and Subtitle

This is not necessarily the finished title but something to work with. Including a tag line (or subtitle) is a great idea. A tag line gives the reader a clear indication of how they are going to benefit from reading your book. Having a working title and tag line gives you something to tell people when you talk about the book you're writing. When you tell people about your book, always start with title – it's the best way to gauge people's interest in your story. Think about it like this: If Tolkien told you he was working on a book titled *The Lord of The Rings*, you'd likely have some good follow-up questions because your interest is piqued. However, if he said the title was *A short guy finds a ring that his uncle owned and has to destroy it in a big volcano with the help of another short guy and then a weird short guy later on*, you wouldn't really have any questions left to ask.

If you find yourself having to explain exactly what the book is about, you may have been too gimmicky, used industry jargon or been too clever.

Define your target market

Clearly define your target market in three to four paragraphs. This will ensure that you truly understand who you are writing for. It is also worth having a reminder on your office wall to keep you focused on exactly who this book is for.

What is the central question that this book is going to answer for readers?

This is perhaps one of the most important parts of your book pitch. If you cannot clearly identify what your reader's central question is, then you may end up writing a book for you, the author, not the reader. There is little point in writing a book about what you think is needed. You need know the types of questions your readers have/will have. What things are keeping them up at night?

Consider Tim Ferris when he wrote the 4-Hour Work Week. He was aiming to help people get smarter at their work, not encourage them to work 60 hours per week to be successful.

How have you tested your central question with your target market?

This is the stage where you approach your target market and ask your central question. This is an important stage as you may be planning a book that doesn't meet the needs of your reader. There is no point writing a book solely on dieting if your target market wants to know how to keep the weight off after they have dieted. There are numerous ways to conduct this research, and this will depend on who your target market is.

You can try:

- Surveys
- Interviews
- Networking groups
- Client data base

What is the book about?

In four to five concise paragraphs, clearly define what this book is all about.

What makes this book unique?

Read other books on your book topic – as many as possible. It's not cheating; it's valuable research. If your direct competitor has written a book, buy it and read it. Find out who the publisher is, and what the book retails for. Also, look at blog posts, news articles and any other written material. This will clearly indicate whether there's something missing from the market and how you can make your book different. Remember, you are unique, and you are writing this book from your own unique, individual experiences.

What is the ultimate benefit to your readers?

As a writer, you need to inspire the reader with a promise of what reading this book will deliver. Having a clearly defined ultimate benefit will help you achieve this. When they've finished your book, is the reader excited and ready to move forward, or are they overwhelmed and confused? If it's the latter, you've done something wrong.

What other books on this topic are there on the market?

Do not skimp on this research. Having a complete understanding of the competition, including their strengths and weaknesses, will help you write a better book. Very few nonfiction books have no competition, and if your topic is particularly tightly niched (e.g., a knitting manual for unicorn farmers), you may need to question if there is a market for your book. If there is little competition, then it's even more important that your market research is extensive. Don't limit yourself to books; Google your topic and the problem it solves.

About the author

This is the time to sell yourself. Tell your readers why they can trust you. This is when we need to tell Boris to take a hike again, as it's sometimes very difficult not to second guess yourself here. I have known some wonderful, highly intelligent, well-educated people who struggle to sell themselves. But this is the time to do just that, both to the reader and to yourself.

Establishing credibility as a non-fiction author is essential, so don't hold back. You may have been fascinated by your subject as a child or writing about your topic for decades. If you're a regular spokesperson in your industry or the media calls you up to comment on a news story, your readers will want to know.

Draft Contents Page

This is where you clearly outline what it is you are going to cover in your book. This is where the work you have already done planning your contents will be invaluable. This pitch document is still only a draft, and you can add and delete when the writing process begins. Things to consider when working on your contents page:

- Write creative chapter titles.
- Break your book into segments or parts.
- Include an introduction.

Also add the details and a page for the About the Author, acknowledgements and index, glossary, additional references or reading links if you are having these.

NOTE: This pitch document is for commercial purposes and maybe you need to pitch to an agent or traditional publisher, in which case your draft contents page is critical. But your book plan (what we worked on earlier) is what you'll use to write your book. Don't use this pitch document to reinvent that.

How are you going to promote your book?

There is no point writing this book unless you clearly understand how you are going to promote it. Ideally, the promotion starts now, while you are writing the manuscript. As soon as you start the book pitch, tell people what you're doing. It is amazing how compelled you are to follow through with writing if you actually tell people. One quick and easy way to begin this promotion is to include the working title and publish date on your email signature. Write blog posts about your book, and either use content that is being included or blog about the writing process. Do a mind map on all the ways you can promote your book. Think about your networks. Which associations do you belong to, social media groups, email lists? Do you write for any media networks? The clearer you are on these sources the easier it is to begin promoting your book, and it is never too early to start.

This week, review your whole plan and your pitch document so you stay focused on what your original plan was, who you want to reach, and why. By having defined your purpose and having thought through all the questions that your readers might want answered, your content will be directed at 'that person', each and every one of them.

This makes your entire manuscript more likely to be 'fit for purpose' and truly enjoyable to read. The more connected your readers feel to what you write, the more likely they are to:

- Finish the whole book.
- Act on what you write.

NOW, take a deep breath, fire up your computer, sharpen your pencils, grab a coffee, and adjust the height of your chair. Set a timer for how long you'll write for each sitting – be it daily, weekly, morning, nightly, afternoon, before breakfast… whenever *your* ideal writing schedule is going to be – and focus on which chapter you'll write this week.

Congratulations! It's time to WRITE your manuscript!

Part 2

Writing Your First Draft

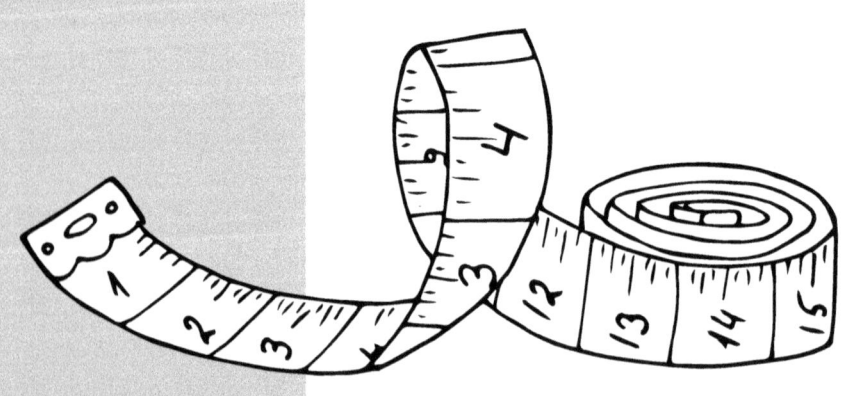

First...the BIG Question of Size

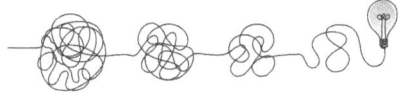

Books are getting smaller, and how your readers want to digest content is changing. We've noticed the need to have shorter chapters in many of the books we're producing now, as well as the need to break up long pages of text with quotes, images, diagrams, and a range of fonts and different visual layouts. Big, long books are often not read to the end, and your objective is to have readers digest all your content, so that they value it and refer your book to others.

A book with approximately 10 chapters, each 2,500–3,000 words, will be roughly 25,000–35,000 words when finished. This will equate to approximately 140–220 pages, depending on formatting. But a non-fiction book that is only 100 pages will not work any less hard for you, the author, or be of less value to your reader. The formula I've outlined in this book for a manuscript will mean your book ends up anywhere from 100–200 pages on average, but there are many variables. This book is likely to be around 100 pages when finished, but it's loaded with content that will be of value to the reader because I have kept the content focused. I've got another book, *Idea to Authority*, which is about getting from conceptual stage all the way through to marketing a finished product. But this one is a short book because I want to ensure you get busy quickly and stay excited about writing your own stuff, easily and well.

This book is specifically for the impatient reader, which comes back to knowing my target market. The central question you want answered is,

'*How can I get my great content out of my head quickly and easily so I can turn it into a book?*'

Some content really does need to be divided across a series of books. In many instances, the reader will want the short, sharp version and can't guarantee they'll finish a big book because they just don't read that many big books. Think about it. When was the last time you read an epic-length (200,000 words) book? What about the one before that? People mostly read on beaches, trains, and on planes, or listen to audio books while traveling, so help your readers out by keeping things snappy.

Other great short books on the market include:
- Who Moved My Cheese?, by S. Johnson (97p)
- Fish!, by S. Lunden, H. Paul, and J. Christensen (116p)
- Of Mice and Men, by J. Steinbeck (137p)
- The Old Man and the Sea, by E. Hemingway (146P)
- Animal Farm, by G. Orwell (118p)
- A Christmas Carol, by C. Dickens (106p)
- Practice the Pause, by V. Gupta (85p)
- The Art of War, by Sun Tzu (42p)

Writers Block

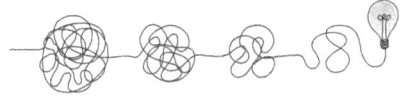

Yes, it's real! Writer's block can be debilitating. Many of us find entirely new ways to procrastinate over our intended work. We raid the pantry, run to the store for extra stationery, or get stuck on YouTube loops until dinner time.

The way I get around writer's block is to keep writing and see what comes up. Neil Gaiman has a great quote about this:

 'You have permission to not write, but you don't have permission to do anything else.'

He's got a point. Just stick with it and keep writing anything that comes to mind, even if it's absurd or irrelevant, because eventually you'll get back in the groove. **The answer is simply to write!** Write words and see what comes up. Just start with a question in your mind and see if you can answer it. Write a verse, rewrite something else to unlock your writer's mind, and then circle back to what you are really wanting to write about.

Having a book plan in this style also helps enormously, as you can immediately dig into a different chapter or piece and go back to the hard parts later. You don't have to write in chronological order either. Find what you most want to write about in the moment and start writing words. The good stuff will flow, I promise you.

Another trick is to plan regular writing time, and be kind to yourself about your productivity. You don't have to be brilliant every time you write something. Just write. Do it regularly and set yourself deadlines. For example, 1,000 words at a time. A chapter a day or week. A 30-minute, one-hour, or half-day block.

Whatever works for you, do that.

Word vs Google Docs

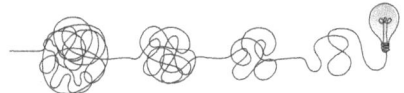

Most editors will usually be quite firm about specifying working with Word files, not Google Docs, Pages, or any other, more unusual options.

Microsoft Word is a good program to use and has some fantastic pre-formatting options. When I'm coaching clients through the writing process, I like to pre-format everything in Word straight away so authors can see where the gaps are, what the page count starts to look like, and how much tidying something needs. I can't tell you the number of times I've formatted something for an author to say, 'Wow, I didn't realise how much I'd rambled here.'

It's completely normal to become impassioned by your work and write huge swaths of content in a single sitting. I encourage this! But often authors need reminding that a book is not an essay, and clear points made quickly and well are not only easier to read, but they look significantly better on a page than wall-to-wall text.

This also helps with the formatting when you send it to your typesetter, so they can see easily where you want things like bolding, headlines, subtitles, emphasis points, or pull quotes.

A pre-edited version is also going to be helpful for sending to your beta readers, so they too can start to see it as a book, not just a collection of articles, blogs, or A4 pages.

Google Docs is a preference for many writers too because they can work on their edits at the same time as their editors, and/or publishing coach. Google Docs is also a free software, and not everyone has Word or likes using it. I've heard of some writers sharing their Google Docs files with beta readers so that they can all see what each other comments on and suggests changes to. This might be a great option for some books, especially collaborative books. However, you can quickly lose track of what you want and don't want in your contents if you get too loose with how and where you share your first draft.

It's worth noting that writing your first draft in programs such as PowerPoint (yes, I once had an author present me with a whole manuscript in PowerPoint and, trust me, it took a lot of undoing to get that file ready for anything!) and simple text files are challenging for parts of the process like pre-formatting, editing, and then subsequent designing.

Word is an industry standard for many reasons. Bear that in mind before exploring too far past that option.

TIP: Always check with your editing team before deciding on using an alternative to Word.

Sharing Your Work

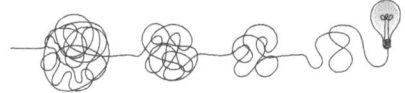

There will be times you'll want or need to share your manuscript. It might be with your book coach, editor, or test readers. Maybe you're collaborating with other authors, which can be a great thing to do for first-time authors in every genre.

Always keep a backed-up copy of your latest version with a fresh name or file number and still download and share as Word files.

Your final version might end up being very different to your early documents. But you may, in fact, want to review old sections or variations, so keep them all. I recommend not deleting any of your previous iterations until you're well and truly satisfied that you've finished with them – and this is likely long after your book is published. Naming them as V.1, V.2, V.3 and so on, with new dates each time, is an easy option and does help with overall file management.

Titles & Subtitles

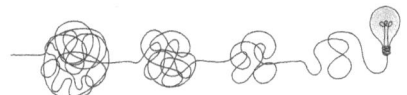

Starting with no title is not the end of the world, but you do need to work through a process for determining your best titles and subtitles. Some authors think they must start with the titles and chapter headings first, but this is not so.

Here' s my three-step process on how to identify and test your title and subtitles .

1. Write 20 potential subtitles – short descriptions of your book, how it answers a central question for your readers, how it can be explained if you said, 'My book is about…' – and put that list on the fridge for a few days.

2. Drop that list down to 10 subtitles and then systematically remove the ones you like the least at the end of every day. See what you have left after a week. Do some extra research on keywords around your topic and see if there are any other ideas to add to or take from that list.

3. When you are happy with a solid list of six, then take that list and share it with your friends. Maybe run a poll on social media and see what suggestions or favourites come back. You may find a couple of amazing new ideas spring forth from these people and one (or even two) may be a clear winner.

 START WITH A DRAFT

Take the top three and decide which one you like best for your main subtitle, and use the others for your marketing, headline on the back cover, or on your social media posts.

The other thing that this exercise will give you is an opportunity to start engaging with people about your book. If you've got a good network and you're writing something of quality, people will want to know more about your book and launch time frame. As these people will go on to become your purchasers, it's a great idea to keep them involved in your process. Some people may also be available to help promote it when the book is ready to launch.

You may also find that your ideas for the main title come clear through decisions made about your subtitles.

TVF WORKSHEET #3

Title & Subtitle Planning

Start with 10-20 descriptions of your book, break this down to six for testing.

Don't Stay Stuck!

If you're struggling to get through this starting point, or somewhere along the way you just wished someone would do this for you, then here's your solution: talk to us. **My team and I do this every day.** We get that not everyone is able to devote the time and skills required for writing their own book. But that doesn't mean you have to hold back on getting your content out there. Book a time to talk with us about what you need the most help with.

www.calendly.com/thewordwitch/curating-content-support

Some of what we can do to help:

- Working through a strategy session with you to get all this content material and book planning done.

- Offering you coaching to get it done yourself.

- Writing your book for you or in collaboration with you to ensure it's still your book, but we'll do the heavy lifting for you to get the first draft finished and ready for editing, production, and design.

Perfection Kills Creativity

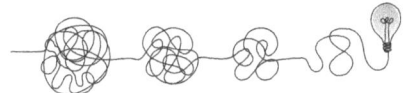

Forget about perfecting your writing as you go!

By the time you get to your third or fourth chapter, you'll need to be reminded to let go of perfectionism. How you write your book will be based on the following process:

Work on the plan and choose which chapters you wish to write. You can do this in any order you like because that's how the plan is set out. You might want to tackle the easy ones first and hold off on the more challenging ones till after you've passed the halfway mark. That's fine. The chapters that need extra research, thinking, or resources can wait. The psychological value of having a few chapters done before you get to the hard stuff is not to be underestimated.

As you finish each chapter draft, share them with your coach if that's what you've arranged, but put the **majority of their feedback on hold** until you finish the entire manuscript.

- When you have finished the whole manuscript in first draft form, then and only then read the whole thing as a completed project.
- Fine-tune from that before you give it to beta readers.

That's the big picture view, but please note that you need to resist the desire to polish up what you've written so far. Just let it go and keep focused on writing your next chapter. That is all.

> **Don't keep this a secret...tell people you are writing a book.**

It keeps you accountable to yourself to have other people know you're undertaking this project. They will ask how it's going and encourage you to keep going when you get distracted.

This week – make it your priority to tell at least two people about your book and ask them to hold you accountable to this project. Perhaps one of these people will be a coach or a mentor, someone who you commercially rely on and pay for their input. Your publishing coach will know exactly how to help you through specific parts of this journey, whereas a mentor might be someone who has also written books and can encourage you along the way.

If your budget or resources don't stretch to a paid coach, then find someone you know will support you, check in with you, and perhaps be prepared to review your content as you write this first draft. Spouses, colleagues, children and close friends are all great options.

Everyone needs a cheerleader – so go find yours.

Writers are Readers

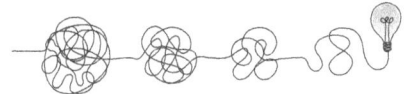

It's very simple. The more you read the better your writing will be. Reading what others are writing in your genre, and on your topic, is an important part of your planning. You also need to see what readers are saying about authors you are competing against or sharing a bookshelf with. So, check out Amazon Reviews. See what books are currently launching, how long they've been out, and how many reviews and comments each has.

The power of storytelling cannot be underestimated when it comes to writing your book, and the best storytellers are also readers. So, what do you spend time reading? If it's mainly instruction manuals, newspapers, or road maps, then you might want to rethink your objectives with writing a book, even if it's a non-fiction book focused on instruction.

To make your facts 'sticky', you must create a story to ensure the memorability of the facts. And the best way to learn good storytelling is to read good stories.

This week – set some time aside to think about the books you most love to read. What makes them good? Chances are they have easily digestible content in short stories. Make a list of your favourite authors. Consider what you love most about them. Read your copy of *Authority Island* if you have not yet done so. After all, I wrote it especially for you to demonstrate the power of disguising instruction in stories.

You'll find the link to 'Authority Island' and 'From Idea to Authority' in the last few pages of this book.

Author Quicksand

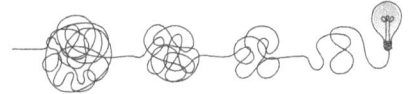

Six Common Mistakes and How to Avoid Them

I've met so many authors experiencing angst and frustration from really just a handful of pitfalls.

I won't lie and say that this journey is free from peril; some of the challenges you face may feel overwhelming. Yet, the majority of problems you'll encounter can likely be traced back to one of these six, and none is as troublesome as they first appear. Just like quicksand, they won't kill you. But knowing how to avoid or deal with them is an indispensable bit of knowledge to have when heading out on this adventure.

1. **Not thinking about their market, their readers.**

This is marketing 101. Who do you want to reach? Why them, and why should they care about what you're sharing? Who are they, where do they hang out, and what do they invest their time and money in, or attention on? You need answers to all of these questions to create an effective call to action. The sooner you come up with those answers, the easier it will be to write something successful.

2. **Not having a plan for what content to write.**

If you spend some time planning what content to share, where it goes, how it flows, and how you wish to present it, you will develop a usable writing plan. This is about ensuring you share the *right* amount of information with appropriate content in a book that is neither too long nor too short. Ensure your chapters are of consistent length and the relevance of your content is explained in ways your readers want to engage with. Some authors come to me having already written a manuscript that is missing vital points, or that lacks key descriptions. Some books are far, far too long and can easily be reworked into two or three books covering different topics.

3. **Not treating their book project as a 'project'.**

Like any project, this requires not only a plan but also KPIs and points of reference along the way. You need a solid overview of what the finished project will look like. Treating your writing as a *well-orchestrated project* requires that you follow points 1 and 2: understanding your market, and having a plan. Don't just sit down and start to write.

4. **Not having a good call to action for readers when they finish their book.**

Do you want to start a movement or change the way people think? What do you want to have happen because of writing this book? Decide that at the start, and then you'll know what kind of call(s) to action to put into your book – not just at the end, but in the content itself. You need to guide your readers to act as soon as they finish the book. A good call to action ensures that you get to further engage with them in some way.

5. **Not knowing from the start how to get their book into their readers' hands.**

Marketing a book is not like selling toothbrushes or a timeshare vacation. You need to focus on using the book for building your own brand and enhancing your current marketing profile. Going back to point 1. You need to know who and where your market is. We talk about Five Keys of Authority Mastery in the *Authority Island* book. You need to know these well enough to use them well, often with the help of experts.

6. **Not using the power of storytelling**

The most common mistake that non-fiction authors make is failing to use the power of stories in their content. **Stories make the facts sticky**. That's why we've used storytelling for thousands of years. We remember a story far better than we recall facts and figures. Allowing a story to convey information keeps your readers engaged and gives a much better chance of finishing the book. You must know your market to share the best kind of stories for them and find ways to make your call to action resonate with them.

These SIX most common mistakes authors make are expensive ones. They can negatively impact on your cost of editing, sales, and reviews, and they make the entire project so much harder.

Pre-formatting Your Manuscript

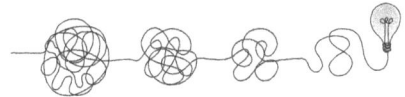

At this stage, your manuscript may still be a collection of individual documents with chapter headings. At some point, you will want to turn this into a document that combines all those chapters and even start thinking about the formatting. This is when it really starts to feel like you're writing a book!

Some tips for pre-formatting:

Set up your Word document as an A5 (14.7x21 cm) or 8.5x5.5 inch document.

Add page numbers and headings. Don't vary your fonts too radically, and don't make it look too fancy or you'll get stuck in the details. Leave the aesthetics to the designers. All you need right now is something that looks like a basic book.

I like to use my standard Styles in Word, and mainly stick with Normal, Heading 1, Heading 2, and Title. Sometimes I'll use a quote or emphasis option. You'll find these options in the tool bar, and you can right-click on each to modify your settings.

You can quickly see what your settings are and what that looks like in the centre window. The Paragraph tab is open from FORMAT at the bottom of the screen.

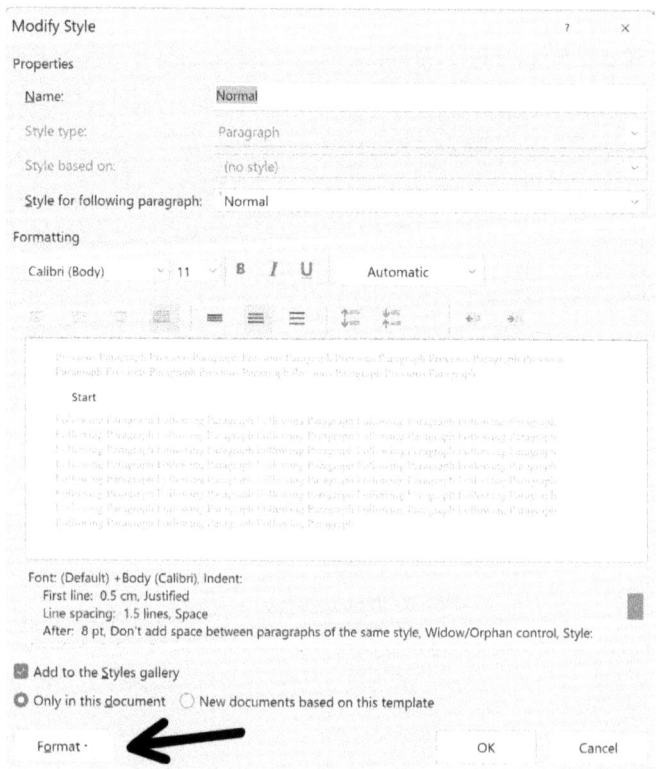

I recommend you set up as follows:

Normal: plain sans-serif font (something more like **ARIAL** and less like TIMES NEW ROMAN, which has serifs on each letter).

Use 11 or 12-point size, and 'first line hanging by 0.5cm', which you will find in the paragraph setting. I also set the line spacing at 1.5, and a small gap after each paragraph so that you don't end up having to use an extra space between paragraphs to separate them. Justify your margins and keep your page numbers in the footer in simple format

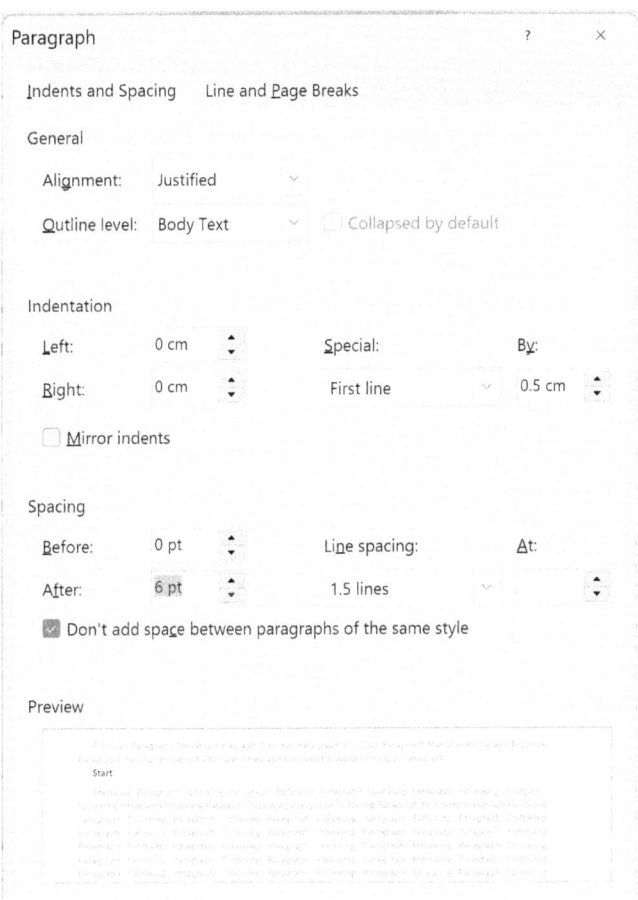

Here's the difference...

What works well:

When the wind blows and the moon rises, the wolf's mood is captured by artists who wax lyrical about the beauty of the wild nights in the desert.

The old cowboys even sing songs about them as they howl through the night and keep them awake, and blah blah blah end of sample text!

Compared with what doesn't:

When the wind blows and the moon rises, the wolf's mood is captured by artists who wax lyrical about the beauty of the wild nights in the desert.
The old cowboys even sing songs about them as they howl through the night and keep them awake, and blah blah blah end of sample text!

One is a lot easier for reading through when you have many pages of similar text.

Set your Heading 1 up as bold, 15pt, centred, with 20pts spacing below. This automatically gets it well above the first line of your chapter text, and Heading 2 as bold, 13 point and 8 points above the next line. Your next line will usually be set to default to 'normal' text when you enter 'return'.

Reserve H1 for chapter headings, and H2 for subheadings. These also means that you can use your Navigation pane (under your View tab) to flick easily between chapters, or even move whole sections around, if needed at any time.

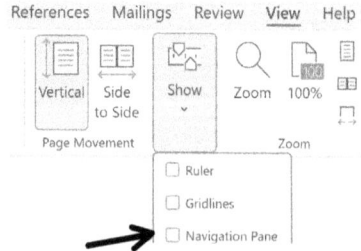

The H1 and H2 settings also enable an easy creation of a contents page which you'll find a link to do under your 'References' tab.

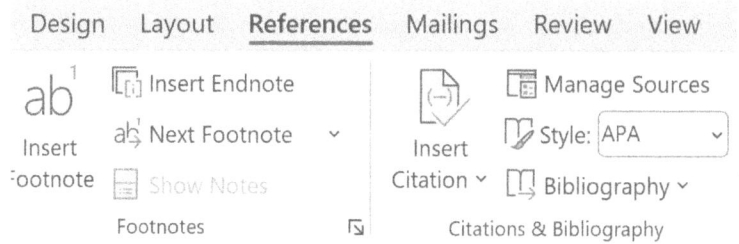

Copy the chapters into their rightful places and number them. Use your styles as set up for headings, subheadings and normal text.

As far as referencing your work, if you know something will need to be checked and referenced, please insert an endnote in your text to remind you to return to that when you are finishing your manuscript. You don't need to get hung up on perfecting the referencing as you go at this stage, as that will slow you down from the necessary 'brain dump' that your first draft needs you to focus on first.

I also use Find and Replace (Ctrl+H) a lot when I'm writing complicated sections and feel I may have overused specific words.

If you are unsure about how to size your margins and pages, use Navigation, or modify your settings. Use your search tool (Alt+Q) in Word and look these up.

Create headings for the front and back matter, such as Biography, Acknowledgements, Foreword, Call to Action, Introduction, or a Sales Page.

Review Your Draft

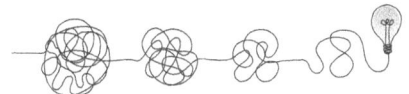

After you have completed the preliminary draft of your manuscript, it's time to turn it over to someone else to take a good look at it. That person may not be your publisher, book shepherd or editor, but they should be able to give you some good feedback on your content. What you are looking for at this stage is assistance in ensuring that your content is complete.

If you are co-authoring a book, one way to ensure a good flow of content is to select parts which each of you will focus on first. Write those, and then swap them so that the other person can review and add content as needed to each section.

With that feedback, you can go back and add what's necessary to complete your manuscript. Leave it for a few days, then give it another thorough review and hand it over for editing.

Let's take your temperature

Rate each question on a 1–5 basis:
5 being VERY much YES, and 1 being NO, not really!

My Manuscript is Ready for Testing because:

I have written approximately 2,000-3,000 words per chapter.	
My chapters are well paced and in good order for my readers to enjoy the flow of my content.	
I have referenced all quotes and reference-required content – or marked where I'm unsure, so that my editor can advise me on this.	
I have read my manuscript and made sure I am 100% happy with the overall content.	
I am okay with it not being perfect yet and understand this is part of the process.	
I have three or four people ready to do a first read, and they understand what is needed from them (and it's not editing or pointing out spelling errors!)	

1–12: Go back and check what you might be able to add or expand on. Read it through again from start to finish. You may need to assess whether you're overthinking your need for perfection too.

13–23: You're probably overthinking it, but recheck your manuscript and read it out loud if you're still unsure where the gaps are.

36–50: You're ready. Line up the test pilots (beta readers) so you can get some feedback that enables you to fine tune and finish your draft before sending it to an editor.

Your Test Pilots

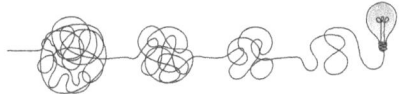

Maybe they're friends, family, colleagues, or other writers. Maybe they're perfect strangers. But often the best people to have on your team are fans of your books/work. Find people who will give you straight-up advice and feedback about what they do and don't like about your manuscript. You can recruit fans in all sorts of ways. I get mine through my social media accounts. When I've finished a manuscript, I post about it and ask for beta readers.

The value of having a good team of 10–12 readers is the fresh eyes on your manuscript. Even your editor and publishing coach can end up getting too close to your work to see missing or overplayed parts.

Beta readers' commitment and responsibility

Invite them to tell you what they do and don't like, and what they would suggest you add, change, or think about. Invite beta readers to review your manuscript formally with a letter outlining your expectations. This shouldn't cost you anything, but you can still profit from selecting good beta readers by offering an advance look at your latest work in progress, and possibly even a small acknowledgement in the back. Watch that person become the biggest champion of your book on release just because you made them feel valued and involved.

Set a date that you would like their feedback by.

There is an example you can download. Use this as a guide to creating your own cover letter to ensure you have educated your beta readers about exactly what is expected of them.

Beta readers may offer editing tips and tell you about the mistakes you still have in your manuscript, and that's great, but keep in mind that these are likely not professionals, and their opinions are less useful to you than their specific critiques. Look for a pattern in their feedback. If seven out of ten readers say that your first chapter is too long compared to the rest of the book, or that you've used the phrase, 'In my opinion...' too much, that's likely something to action.

Forewarn them that the manuscript is in the draft stage and that errors *will be there* for finding. Remind them before they start that editing and proofing are not what you're seeking, but that all errors will be gratefully noted.

Remember to thank them for their time and response. You might put this into the acknowledgements, or send them a personal note and a printed, autographed copy of your book when it is published. Invite them to the launch if you know when that is. Don't forget to ask them to please post a review on Amazon, Goodreads, and other online resellers if they like the book.

Finally, a note of warning: you must be thick skinned if you want objective feedback. Some people prefer to invest in a formal manuscript review, which is a paid service by publishing and author service providers. However, I still recommend going through this stage of writing and getting feedback before investing in that option.

You may want to also repeat this process if you find that you have had so much great feedback that you wish to do some very heavy rewriting before finishing your draft and preparing for an editor to take a look.

 YOUR TEST PILOTS

Beta Reader Invitation - Template

New Message

To

Subject Join my Beta Reader Team for {BOOK TITLE}!

Hi {ADD NAME},

As you know, I decided this year would be THE year for me to finally write my first book: {INSERT YOUR TITLE}!

I've been working hard on it for a few years now (its morphed along the path), and happy to say I've written the first draft, and I'm ready to send my manuscript off to a professional editor.

My publishing mentor recommends I share my manuscript with a small team of what she calls 'Beta Readers' who can offer up any final comments before my book gets published and I picked you.

Thanks for agreeing to become one of my **Beta Readers**. The responsibility is relatively light.

Here's how it works:
I have attached my completed manuscript, prior to final editing. You read it, give me back some comments in terms of:

- ✓ Let me know what you liked
- ✓ Share what you think is underdeveloped or overexplained
- ✓ Suggest any changes you'd recommend

No need to proofread—this is an early draft, and professional editing will come later. However, if you spot anything major, feel free to mention it.

From there, I take that feedback, finalise my manuscript draft, and proceed with the publishing process.

Next Steps:
If you're in, please send me your feedback by **{SPECIFY A DATE, e.g., June 12th}**. I truly appreciate your time, and to say thank you:

📖 Your name will be included in the acknowledgments

📖 You'll receive a signed, printed copy when it's published

★ If you enjoy the book, I'd love for you to leave a brief Amazon review and share it with others

I know life gets busy, so if this isn't the right time, no worries—just let me know. Thanks so much for considering this!

Thanks so much,
{YOUR NAME}

You may not like a critique, but it's worth having. Following the feedback, you will have additional writing and editing to do. But chances are, you will also have a much better book.

Resource Reminder – you can easily access the full set of templates featured in this book, and some bonus ones too, simply by visiting: **www.indieexpertspublishing.com/startwiththedraft**.

Don't Stay Stuck

If you're struggling to get through this starting point, or somewhere along the way you just wished someone would do this for you, then here's your solution: talk to us. **My team and I do this every day.** We get that not everyone is able to devote the time and skills required for writing their own book. But that doesn't mean you have to hold back on getting your content out to your market. Book a time to talk with us about what you need the most help with.

Front and Back Matter

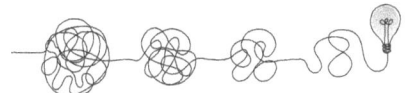

This book is primarily about getting your contents drafted and ready to hand over to an editor, then your production people. But it's worth noting that you will also need to consider these parts of your book.

An acknowledgements page at the back of your book, which is ideally about 500 words. Think of it like an Oscar Acceptance Speech. Keep it brief but don't forget to thank the necessary people, including beta readers and your editors.

Your bio needs to be about you professionally yet not read like a CV. Again, this goes at the back of the book, and including a quality author photo with it is a very good idea.

A simple foreword may be something you want to have, but it's not critical to your book. If you know someone who is ideal to write this for you because they have relevant expertise, invite them to do so. They may prefer to simply review your book or write a recommendation rather than a whole foreword.

Your sales page, also called the Call-to-Action page, is where you want readers to go to discover their next steps and get more of what you're offering. This page will also have your social media links or addresses, and perhaps feature a free resource they can access from your website with instructions and a link to get this .

But wait, there's more!

There are several more things you'll need to work through as part of your front and back matter, but this is not the book for that in-depth information. However, if you wish to access my book From *Idea to Authority*, you'll find all that information there. For even more in-depth premium resources check out the Indie Experts website. These resources have been created for authors wanting to do all their own writing and publishing with support and resources. Details are on my own Call-to-Action see page 91.

What to do next...

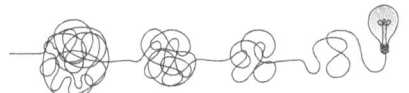

Dear Author,

You might think that all that hard work means you're ready to publish your book, but you do still have a lot of work to do. The writing of your manuscript is a major undertaking and for that you have my congratulations. Now, you need to work with a team to take your book to the next level. I'm talking about editing, design, reviews for marketing, and formatting your files so they can be readily uploaded to various platforms.

If you'd like to simply work through an online APP to get the remainder of your book process underway, I've created videos and bonus help if you need it. But first, I recommend you take some time to consider the following.

Have a conversation with me or one of my amazing team about your next steps. Do you need help identifying and working with an editor? Will you need assistance with design and formatting? What about the actual publishing process, and working through Amazon or Ingram Spark and creating files to upload? Finally, there's the launch and marketing plan to ensure you get your best content out to your identified market.

If you would like to have a conversation with us about how we can either point you in the right direction or roll our sleeves up and walk you through all the next steps, then book a call, using this link, and **we'll ensure you are confidently ready for the Next Steps.**

Dixie

A word about having a team, *vs* doing this on your own.

You can write your first draft on your own using the formula and experience found in these pages. This book is about being able to tap into your best content, and getting it sorted and developed into a book of your own. I hope you've got something useful out of it already.

If you want to do this alone, do that. But if you want to get the best out of your content, you are going to need a bit of help along the way. You'll notice there are references throughout this book to ensure you start thinking early about gathering some extra help, such as editors, designers, coaches, and marketing experts.

You don't have to assemble a team first, but starting to think about those you will need on your authority journey going forward is recommended.

Call to Action

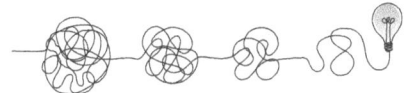

Here's my own Call to Action Page!

As you'll have noticed throughout this book, I've referenced several additional resources you can get here at the end of the book.

Here, you'll find a few bonus tools and links to my other books, which I highly recommend you read as part of your author journey.

BOOKS for AUTHORS:

- **Authority Island** – How some authors become authorities, and others just write books.
- **From Idea to Authority** – Write, Produce and Promote a Nonfiction Book to Market Your Business.

You can access sample chapters to these and other books at **www.dixiecarlton.com/books** and also extra resources for authors at **www.indieexpertspublishing.com**

Specifically if you'd like to download TVF Worksheets, and a helpful document on 'how to write stories and case studies' you can access these free at **www.indieexpertspublishing.com/startwiththedraft**

You can also find access to our Podcast – The Experts Journey, Substack and the Indie Experts YouTube channel at:
www.Linktr.ee/indieexperts

Acknowledgements

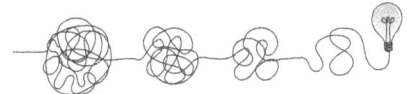

I have a few people who need to be thanked and celebrated for their contribution to this book. First and foremost, to my test pilots and many early readers who have given great feedback to help develop the content into this updated version and thank you so much for taking the time to review, comment, and give me valuable insights into what was still needed. Special mention goes to Alex, Meg, and Nicky – thank you.

Daniela Catucci – another outstanding cover design!

To Rosemary Hepzoden for outstanding editing and feedback as always – I learn so much from you in every conversation – thank you. And Ammie Christiansen for being the best and most fun partner, designer, and working buddy. Your extra design skills and resources in this updated version are breathtaking and I'm so excited about the work we're doing together. Thank you.

And to all my author clients over many years who have helped me develop and refine my resources and learn mastery of my topic through helping them with their books and marketing.

Extra Resources

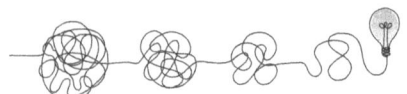

If you need help developing your book, your story ideas, or just some great design and typesetting but are not quite sure where to start, chances are after reading this book you'll have a much better idea of what you need to do.

We can help you with a range of great tools, helpful support and Coaching or Author Services. So reach out and let's have a chat about what you need.

You'll also find easily downloadable versions of some of the many resources we mentioned in the pages of this book too. Head to: **www.indieexpertspublishing.com/StartwiththeDraft**

To invite Dixie to speak at your next event, on Publishing and Marketing, please visit **www.dixiecarlton.com/speaker**

Follow Dixie and Indie Experts on Linkedin, Substack, You Tube, at the following links:

Linktr.ee/indieexperts

About Dixie Carlton

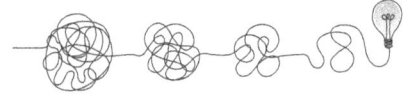

Dixie Maria Carlton is a trailblazer in the world of publishing, marketing, and professional speaking, with a career spanning over two decades. In 2001, after selling her successful promotional marketing company, she found herself at a crossroads. With time to explore new opportunities, she wrote her first book—just as Amazon and the self-publishing revolution were beginning to take shape. This pivotal moment led her to work with a high-profile publishing and marketing expert in the U.S., where she gained invaluable insights into the intersection of these industries.

Since then, Dixie has authored multiple books, earned industry awards, and guided hundreds of professional speakers, CEOs, and industry experts to transform their expertise into impactful, high-quality publications. Her clients, many of whom have become bestselling and award-winning authors, span industries as diverse as IT, security, agriculture, retail, education, mountaineering, and medicine.

A recognized authority in Publishing 3.0, Dixie has represented books at international book fairs in Frankfurt and London, sold foreign rights, and collaborated with leading literary agents and PR specialists. She understands the power of the written word when combined with a strategic approach—helping experts move seamlessly between "Pages and Stages" to build credibility, influence, and business success.

As the creator of the Tri-Variant Framework™ for Content Curation, Dixie believes in the art of storytelling and the science of strategic publishing. She describes her work as "getting paid to deep dive into fascinating lives and topics," and she thrives on helping authors shape their narratives into books that truly make an impact. Whether guiding first-time writers or seasoned professionals, her mission remains the same: to turn great ideas into authoritative books that amplify expertise and open doors.

www.ingramcontent.com/pod-product-compliance
Lightning Source LLC
Chambersburg PA
CBHW061739070526
44585CB00024B/2741